THE OFFICIAL
Manchester United
Mental Maths Book

PAUL BROADBENT

Letts

KICK-OFF

The Manchester United books are a fun way to learn and practise your Maths skills. Each book contains:
11 Big Matches, a flick-a-book player, find the cup, a poster and a board game!

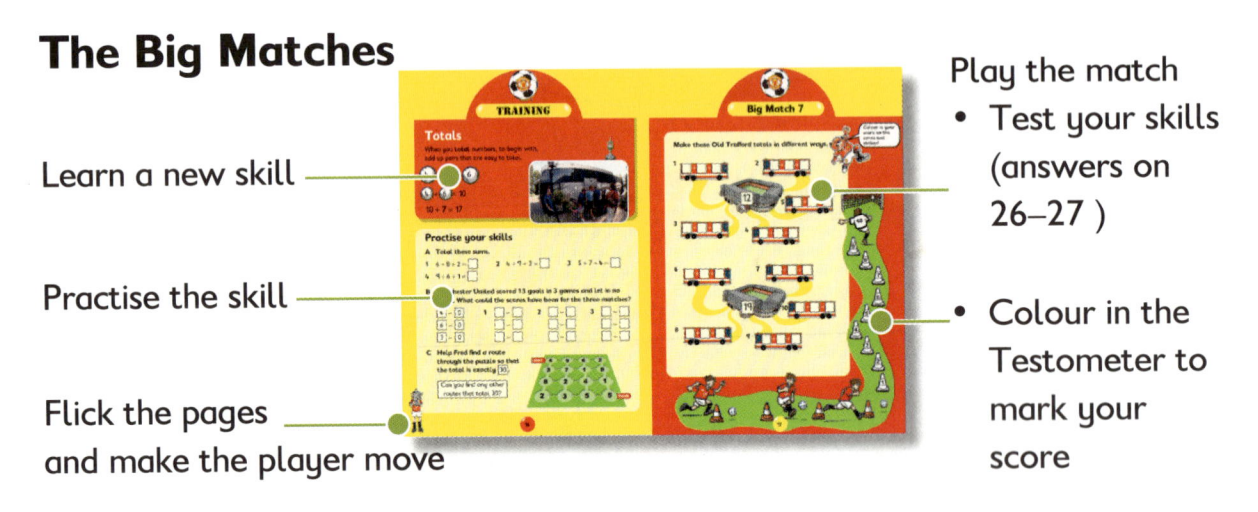

The Big Matches

Learn a new skill

Practise the skill

Flick the pages and make the player move

Play the match
- Test your skills (answers on 26–27)
- Colour in the Testometer to mark your score

See if you can find the cup hidden in each unit!

Enjoy the pull-out game and poster in the middle of the book!

The Game

What you need and how to play

The Poster

Collect all the books in the series and the six individual posters make one big poster!

Contents

Adding to 10 4–5

Taking away 6–7

Finding the difference 8–9

Number facts 10–11

Doubles 12–13

Missing numbers 14–15

Totals 16–17

Giving change 18–19

Decade sums 20–21

Money 22–23

Solving problems 24–25

Answers 26–27

TRAINING

Adding to 10

A number line can be useful when adding on.

Count the jumps.

1 2 3 4 5 6 7 8 9 10

Start at 4 and count on 3.

4 + 3 = 7

Practise your skills

Finish the jumps and write the answers.

1 3 + 5 = ☐

2 4 + 4 = ☐

3 2 + 3 = ☐

4 6 + 3 = ☐

5 5 + 4 = ☐

Big Match 1

Colour in your score on the queuing supporters!

Join the numbers on the shirts to the answers on the number line.

0 1 2 3 4 5 6 7 8 9 10

1 — 3 + 2
3 — 5 + 2
5 — 6 + 3
2 — 4 + 6
4 — 4 + 4

0 1 2 3 4 5 6 7 8 9 10

6 — 3 + 5
8 — 4 + 3
10 — 3 + 3
7 — 5 + 4
9 — 2 + 8

5

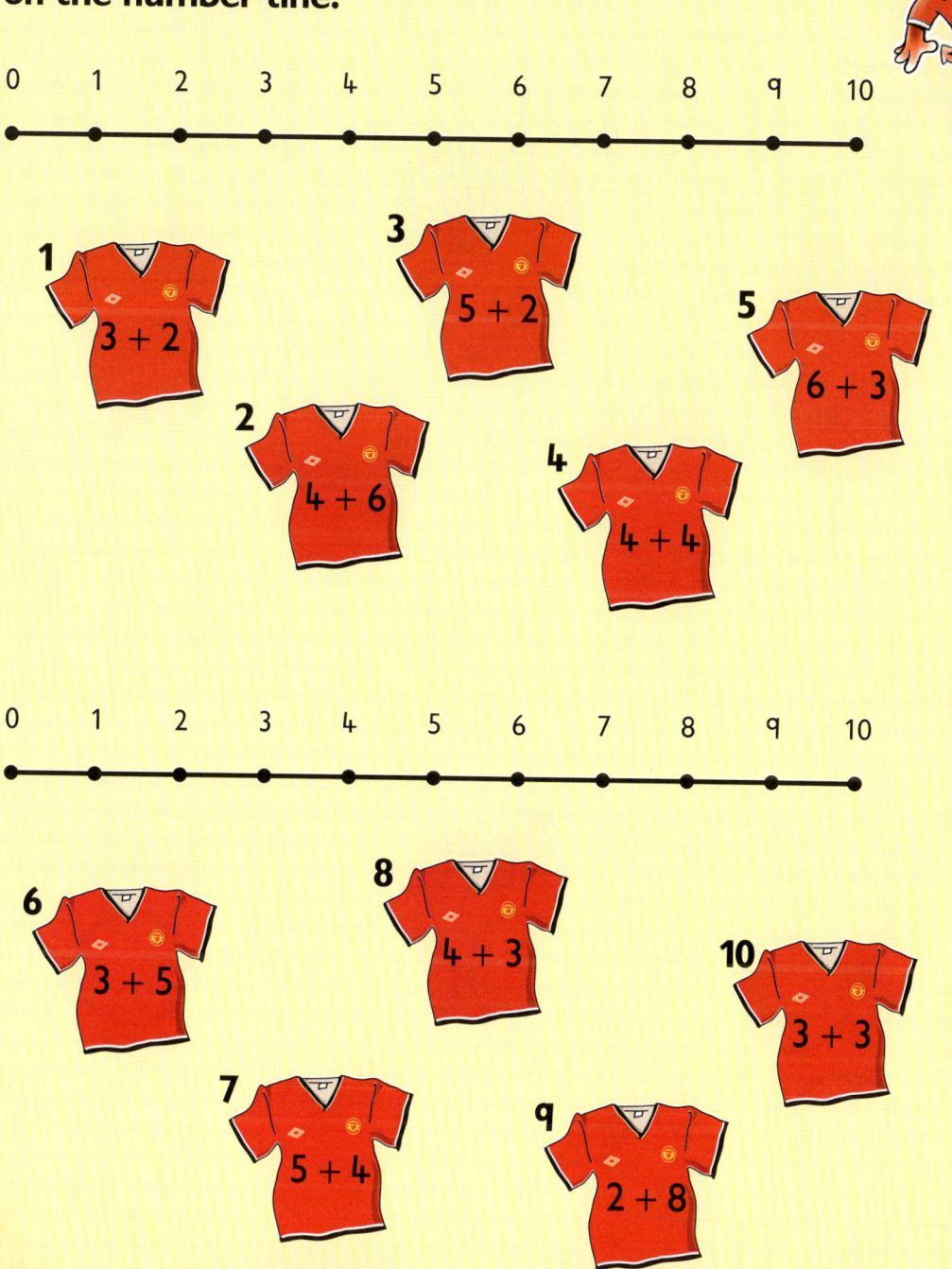

TRAINING

Taking away

It is useful to know the **subtraction facts** for a number.

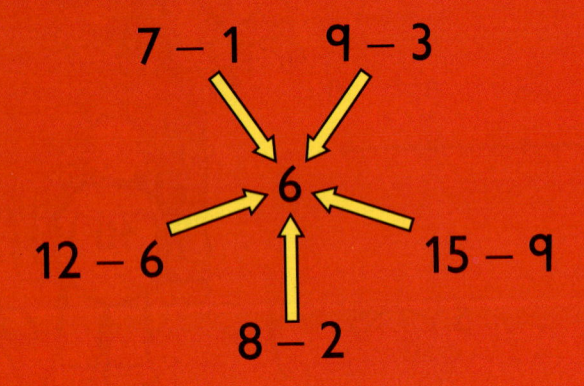

7 – 1   9 – 3
      ↘ ↓ ↙
12 – 6 → 6 ← 15 – 9
        ↑
      8 – 2

These all have an answer of 6.

Practise your skills

A Use taking away facts to find different ways of making the answers in the red footballs.

1   8

12 – 4

2   9

3   5

B Colour the odd one out in each bag.

1
15 – 10
16 – 12
6 – 2
18 – 14
12 – 8
9 – 5

2
17 – 10
20 – 13
8 – 1
15 – 9
19 – 12
11 – 4

Big Match 2

Complete the tables for these number machines.

1

in	13	18		20	
out		7		12	

2

in	20		16		13
out		7		11	

Colour in your score on the shirts!

TRAINING

Finding the difference

To find the difference between two numbers, count on from the lower number.

7 — **11**

What is the difference between 7 and 11?

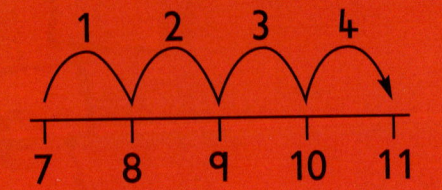

1 2 3 4

7 8 9 10 11

The difference is 4.

11 − 7 = 4

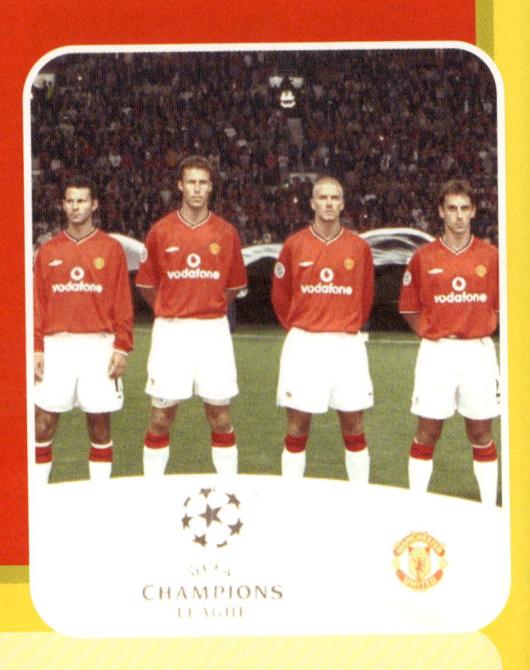

Practise your skills

A Draw the jumps to find the differences.

1 The difference between 3 and 8 is ☐

2 The difference between 4 and 10 is ☐

3 The difference between 5 and 9 is ☐

B Use a ruler. Join up opposite pairs of numbers with a difference of 5 to make a pattern.

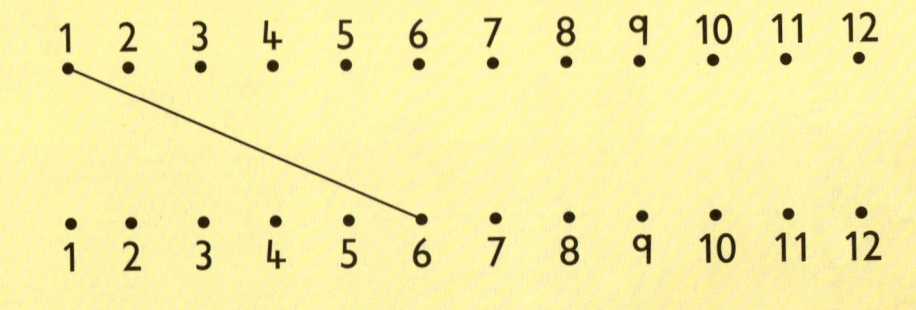

1 2 3 4 5 6 7 8 9 10 11 12

1 2 3 4 5 6 7 8 9 10 11 12

8

Big Match 3

Write the difference between these pairs of numbers.

1. 5, 8 _____
2. 6, 10 _____
3. 9, 2 _____
4. 7, 4 _____
5. 3, 8 _____
6. 12, 5 _____
7. 8, 11 _____
8. 14, 7 _____
9. 15, 9 _____
10. 13, 6 _____

Colour in your score on the exercising players!

TRAINING

Number facts

A **trio** is a set of three numbers which make addition and subtraction facts.
Look at this trio.

4 **3** **7**

4 + 3 = 7   7 − 4 = 3
3 + 4 = 7   7 − 3 = 4

Practise your skills

A Make four number facts for the trio in each goal.

1. (3, 8, 5)

3 + ☐ = ☐
☐ + 3 = ☐
☐ − 3 = ☐
☐ − ☐ = 3

2. (6, 11, 5)

☐ + 6 = ☐
6 + ☐ = ☐
☐ − 6 = ☐
☐ − ☐ = 6

3. (12, 9, 3)

9 + ☐ = ☐
☐ + 9 = ☐
☐ − ☐ = 9
☐ − 9 = ☐

B Follow this number trail. Which number do you reach?

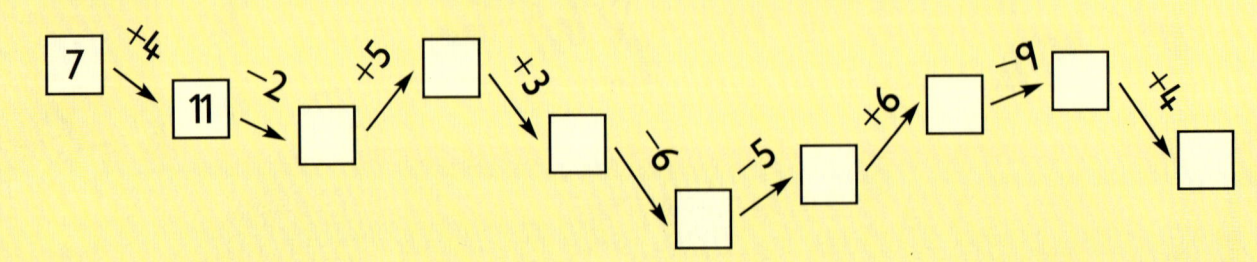

7 →+4→ 11 →−2→ ☐ →+5→ ☐ →+3→ ☐ →−6→ ☐ →−5→ ☐ →+6→ ☐ →−9→ ☐ →+4→ ☐

Big Match 4

Colour in your score on the coaches!

Use pairs of these numbers to complete the trios.

1. ☐ + ☐ = 17
2. ☐ + ☐ = 13
3. ☐ + ☐ = 15
4. ☐ + ☐ = 20
5. ☐ + ☐ = 14

12 6 8
9 7

Use pairs of these numbers to complete the trios.

6. ☐ − ☐ = 5
7. ☐ − ☐ = 9
8. ☐ − ☐ = 12
9. ☐ − ☐ = 3
10. ☐ − ☐ = 8

13 5 17
19 8

The Manchester United Soccer School travels the country to coach children in football skills.

TRAINING

Doubles

If you learn your doubles, you can use this to work out other sums.

4 + 4 = 8   →   4 + [5] is 1 more   →   4 + 5 = 9

Practise your skills

A Write the answer and learn these doubles.

1 + 1 = ☐   2 + 2 = ☐   3 + 3 = ☐   4 + 4 = ☐   5 + 5 = ☐
6 + 6 = ☐   7 + 7 = ☐   8 + 8 = ☐   9 + 9 = ☐   10 + 10 = ☐

B Use the doubles to answer these.

1. 7 + 8
2. 10 + 9
3. 7 + 6
4. 6 + 5
5. 9 + 8
6. 4 + 3
7. 9 + 10
8. 5 + 4
9. 8 + 9

C Look at the answers in question B.
Use the code wheel with your answers to find the names of two strikers.

☐☐☐☐☐ and ☐☐☐☐

Code wheel: 7=C, 15=Y, 11=K, 17=E, 19=O, 5=S, 13=R, 9=L

Big Match 5

Colour in your score on the kit!

Write the numbers coming out of this doubling machine.

1. 6 ☐
2. 8 ☐
3. 7 ☐
4. 11 ☐
5. 9 ☐

Answer these sums.

6. 8 + 7 = ☐
7. 6 + 7 = ☐
8. 9 + 8 = ☐
9. 5 + 6 = ☐
10. 11 + 12 = ☐

TRAINING

Missing numbers

When there are missing numbers in a problem, use the other numbers to help work them out.

5 + ☐ = 8   8 − 5 is 3, so the missing number is 3

☐ − 2 = 4   4 + 2 is 6, so the missing number is 6

Practise your skills

A Look at the pattern in this addition pyramid. Write the missing numbers in the pyramids below.

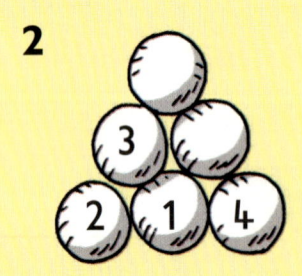

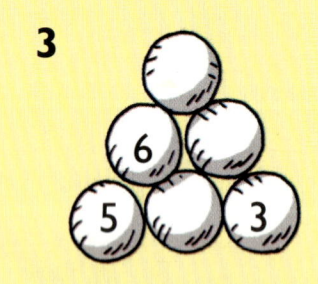

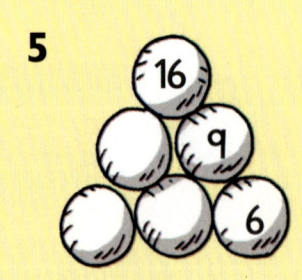

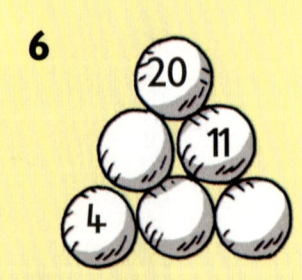

Example pyramid: 11 / 6, 5 / 4, 2, 3

1. Top: ☐; middle: 7; bottom: 3, 1, 6
2. Top: ☐; middle: 3, ☐; bottom: 2, 1, 4
3. Top: ☐; middle: 6, ☐; bottom: 5, ☐, 3
4. Top: 15; middle: 9, ☐; bottom: ☐, ☐, 4
5. Top: 16; middle: ☐, 9; bottom: ☐, ☐, 6
6. Top: 20; middle: ☐, 11; bottom: ☐, 4, ☐

B These players are lost. Write the numbers in the correct place.

Players' numbers: 7, 9, 3, 2, 5, 8

1. 4 + ☐ = 11
2. 8 − ☐ = ☐
3. ☐ + 6 = ☐
4. ☐ − 4 = 5

Good Luck!

4	19	14	20	16	8	12	3
9	2	7	17	5	14	1	13
8	13	15	12	3	18	6	11
3	11	8	9	20	12	16	4
18	9	4	19	5	17	9	7
1	6	14	11	6	4	15	10
7	10	15	18	8	12	2	16
5	12	2	19	17	10	13	6

Manchester United

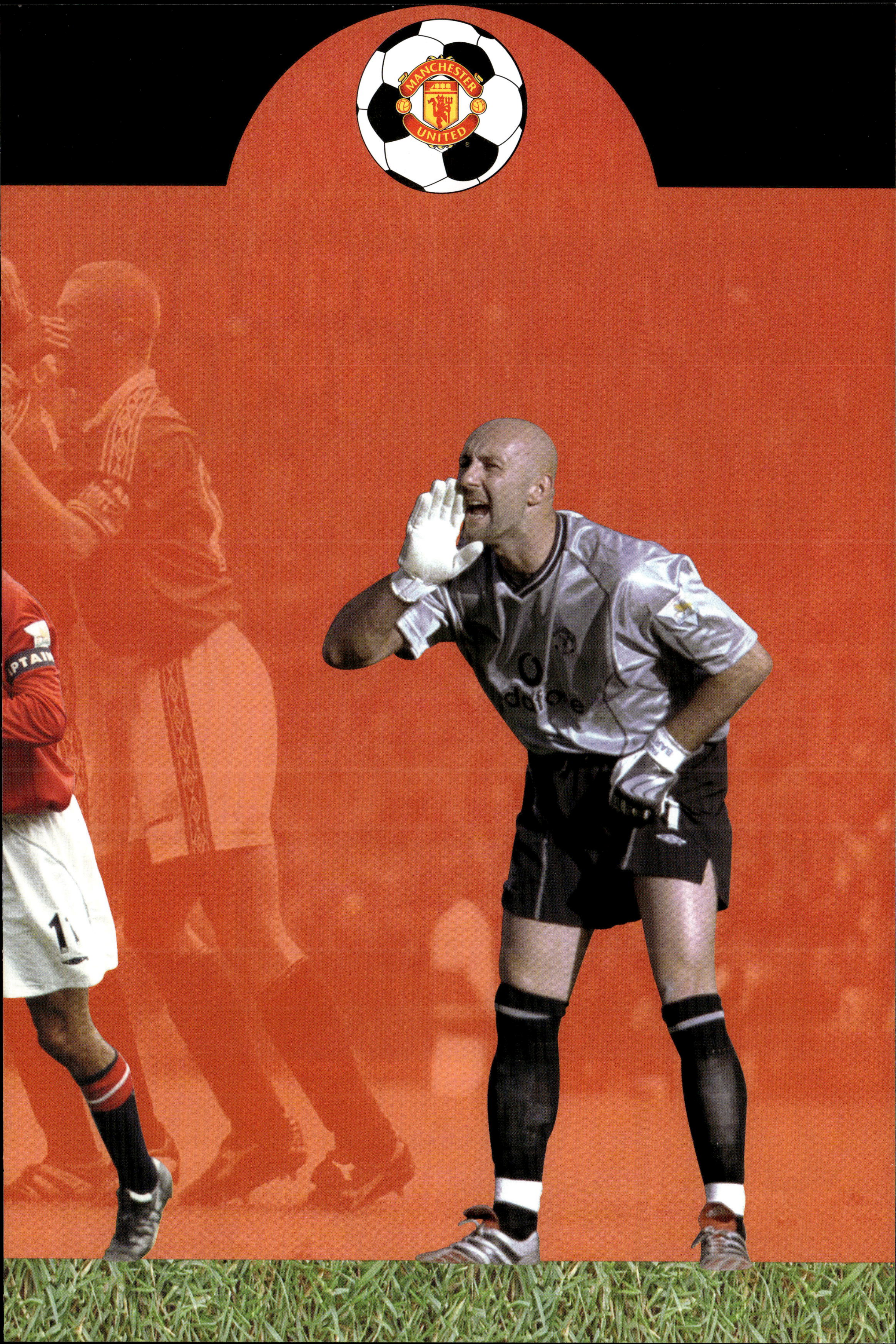

Game

You need:
- 10 number cards, 1–10. Make them from card or used playing cards.
- Some coloured counters or buttons.

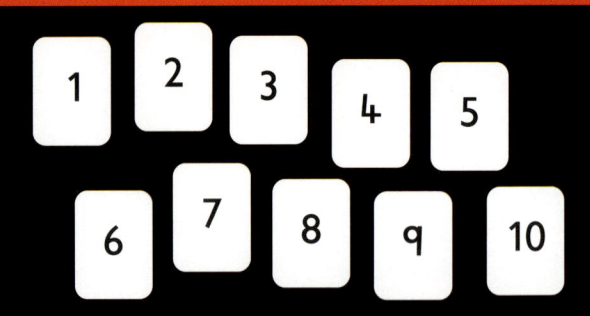

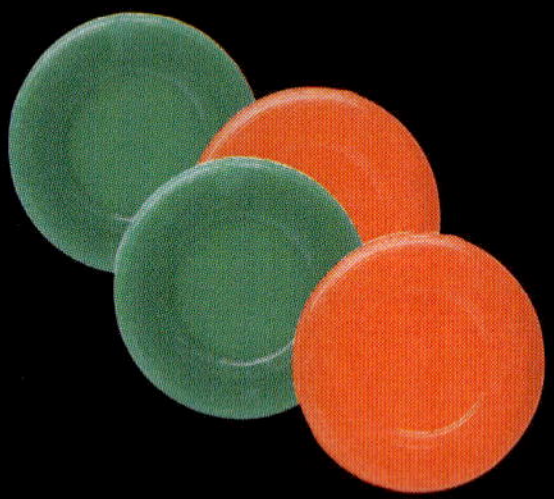

How to play
- The aim of the game is to make a row of four counters in any direction.
- Each player needs different coloured counters.
- Shuffle the cards and turn them face down.
- Player 1 takes two cards and turns them over.

- Choose whether to total the number (15) or find the difference (3).
- Cover one of the chosen numbers on the grid with a counter.
- Return the cards and shuffle for player 2 to have a turn.
- The winner is the player who makes a row of four counters in any direction.

15	12	③
8	9	20

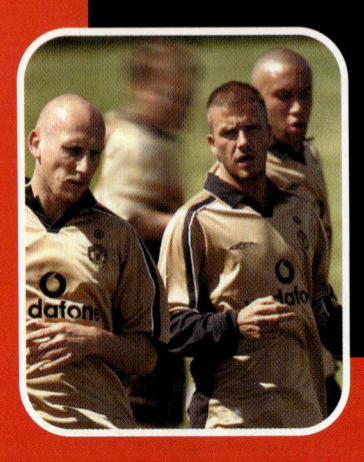

Big Match 6

Write the missing numbers.

1. 8 + ☐ = 10
2. ☐ + 4 = 9
3. 9 + ☐ = 14
4. ☐ + 3 = 12
5. 7 + ☐ = 13
6. ☐ − 4 = 9
7. 8 − ☐ = 5
8. ☐ − 6 = 6
9. 12 − ☐ = 5
10. ☐ − 3 = 8

Colour in your score on the scarf!

There are over 200 official Manchester United FC supporters' clubs found all over the world.

TRAINING

Totals

When you **total** numbers, to begin with, add up pairs that are easy to total.

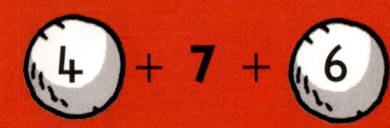

④ + 7 + ⑥

④ + ⑥ = 10

10 + 7 = 17

Practise your skills

A Total these sums.

1. 6 + 8 + 2 = ☐
2. 4 + 9 + 3 = ☐
3. 5 + 7 + 4 = ☐
4. 9 + 6 + 1 = ☐

B Manchester United scored 13 goals in 3 games and let in no goals. What could the scores have been for the three matches?

4 – 0	1	☐ – ☐	2	☐ – ☐	3	☐ – ☐
6 – 0		☐ – ☐		☐ – ☐		☐ – ☐
3 – 0		☐ – ☐		☐ – ☐		☐ – ☐

C Help Fred find a route through the puzzle so that the total is exactly ☐30☐.

Can you find any other routes that total 30?

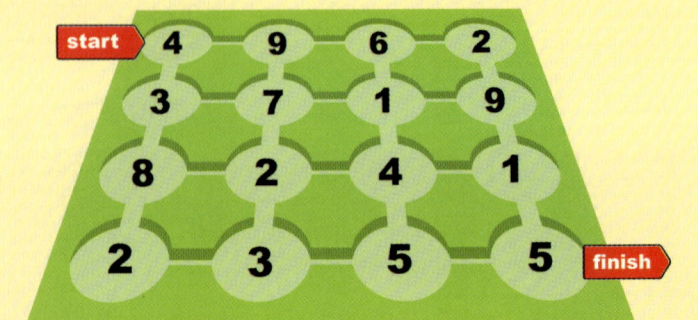

start → 4 – 9 – 6 – 2
        3 – 7 – 1 – 9
        8 – 2 – 4 – 1
        2 – 3 – 5 – 5 → finish

Big Match 7

Make these Old Trafford totals in different ways.

Colour in your score on the cones and striker!

1. ☐ + ☐ + ☐
2. ☐ + ☐ + ☐
3. ☐ + ☐ + ☐
4. ☐ + ☐ + ☐
5. ☐ + ☐ + ☐

12

6. ☐ + ☐ + ☐
7. ☐ + ☐ + ☐
8. ☐ + ☐ + ☐
9. ☐ + ☐ + ☐
10. ☐ + ☐ + ☐

19

TRAINING

Giving change

When you buy things you will sometimes be given some change. To work out change count up from the price to the amount of money you gave.

38p → 40p → 50p

The change is 12p.

Practise your skills

You have 50p to spend. Circle the coins to show the change.

1. 43p   change: ☐ p

2. 35p   change: ☐ p

3. 27p   change: ☐ p

4. 31p   change: ☐ p

Big Match 8

Colour in your score on the MUFC items!

Write the change from 20p for each of these.

1. 17p — change: ☐ p
2. 11p — change: ☐ p
3. 15p — change: ☐ p
4. 14p — change: ☐ p
5. 8p — change: ☐ p

Write the change from £1 for each of these.

6. 65p — change: ☐ p
7. 40p — change: ☐ p
8. 55p — change: ☐ p
9. 48p — change: ☐ p
10. 72p — change: ☐ p

TRAINING

Decade sums

If you know your number bonds, it is easy to add multiples or groups of 10.

10 20 30 40 50
60 70 80 90 100

2 + 3 = 5
20 + 30 = 50

8 + 5 = 13
80 + 50 = 130

Can you see the pattern?

Practise your skills

A Write the missing numbers.

1. 30   60 70

2. 90   120 130

B Join the sums to the correct totals.

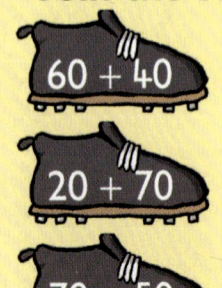

60 + 40
20 + 70
70 + 50
80 + 30
40 + 40

80
90
100
110
120

30 + 70
40 + 50
60 + 60
50 + 30
60 + 50

Big Match 9

Write the totals of these pairs of numbers.

1. 30 + 40 =
2. 20 + 50 =
3. 60 + 30 =
4. 10 + 70 =
5. 20 + 70 =
6. 40 + 70 =
7. 80 + 80 =
8. 30 + 90 =
9. 50 + 60 =
10. 70 + 90 =

Colour in your score on the film of the match!

TRAINING

Money

When you total coins, start with the highest value and go down to the lowest.

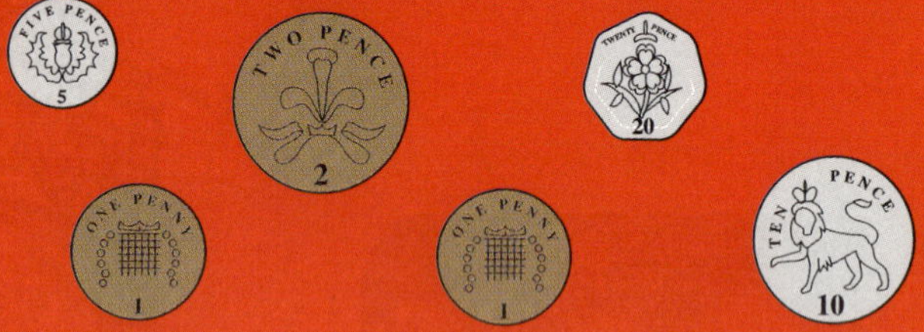

20p + 10p + 5p + 2p + 1p + 1p = 39p

Practise your skills

A Total these amounts.

1. ☐ p

2. ☐ p

3. ☐ p

4. ☐ p

B Draw coins to make each set equal £1.

1.

2.

Big Match 10

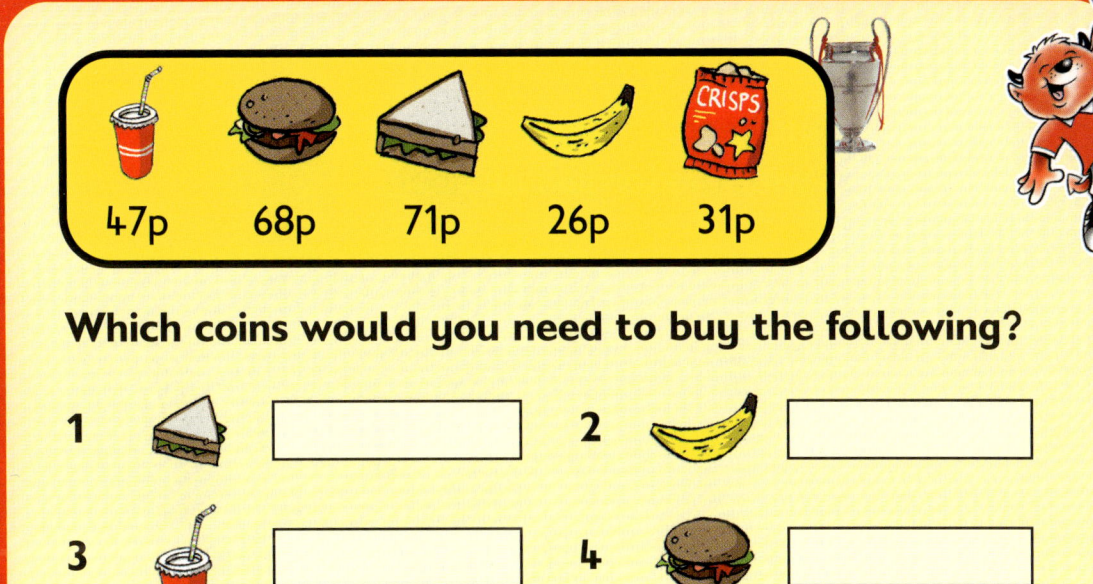

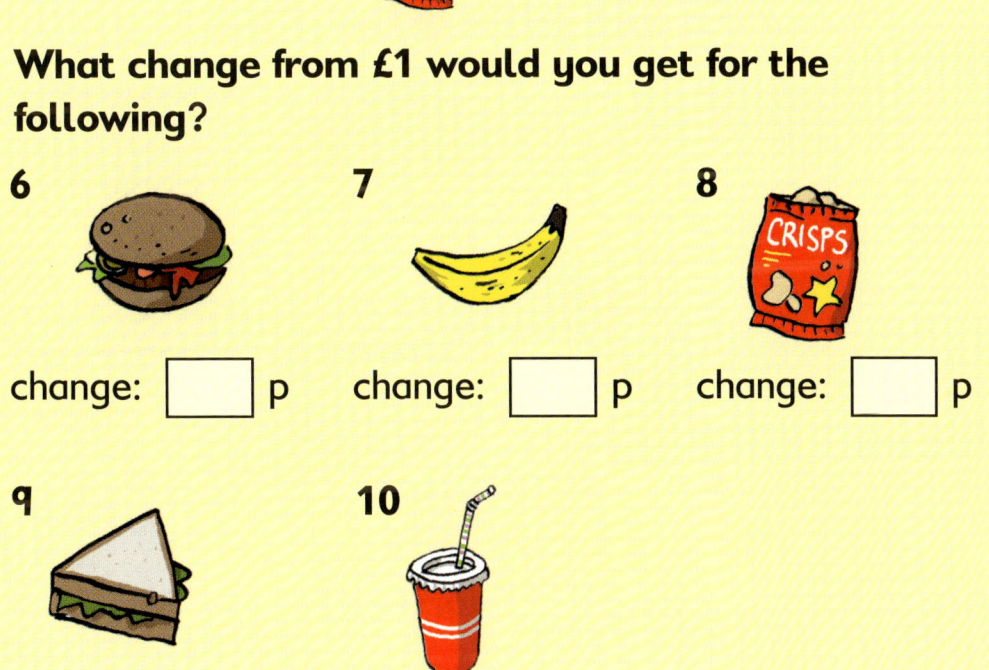

47p 68p 71p 26p 31p

Which coins would you need to buy the following?

1.
2.
3.
4.
5.

What change from £1 would you get for the following?

6. change: ☐ p
7. change: ☐ p
8. change: ☐ p
9. change: ☐ p
10. change: ☐ p

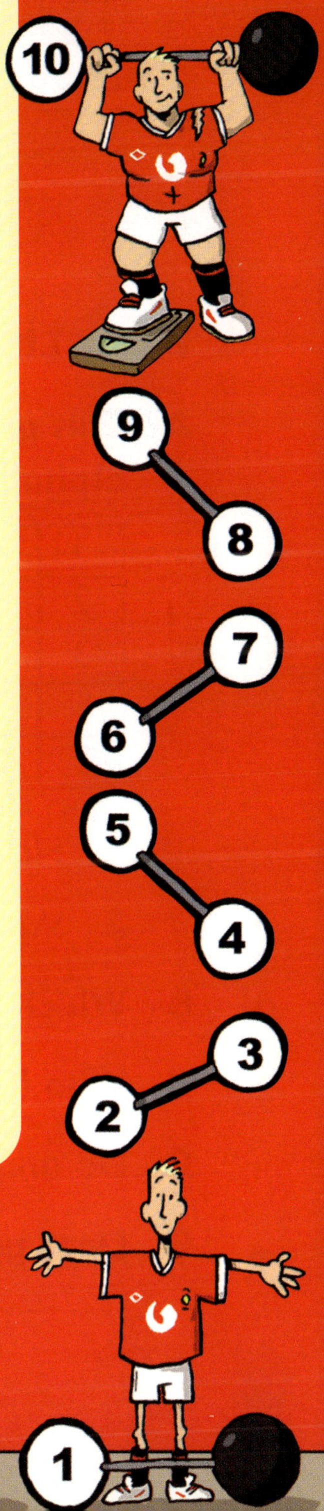

Colour in your score on the weights!

TRAINING

Solving problems

Add numbers carefully in your head.
It sometimes helps to start with the largest number.
These are **addition** words:

- Total
- Sum
- Add
- Altogether

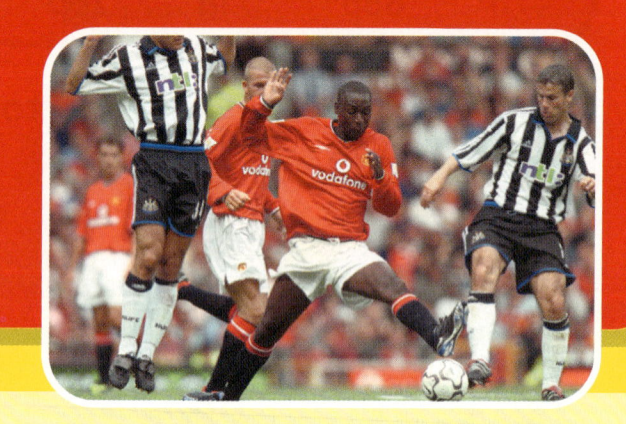

Practise your skills

A This grid shows how much each letter of the alphabet is worth.

1	A	F	K	P	U	Z
2	B	G	L	Q	V	
3	C	H	M	R	W	
4	D	I	N	S	X	
5	E	J	O	T	Y	

COLE is worth
3 + 5 + 2 + 5 → 15

1. How much is BECKHAM worth? ☐
2. What about GIGGS? ☐

B Which Manchester United player is worth the most? _____

C Who has the lowest number of points? _____

D Do any players total exactly 20? _____

E Does your name have the same number of points as any player? _____

Big Match 11

Complete the table showing the number of goals scored by these players in the 1999/2000 season.

David Beckham	9
Andy Cole	24
Ryan Giggs	10
Roy Keane	
Paul Scholes	
Teddy Sheringham	
Ole Gunnar Solskjaer	
Dwight Yorke	

1. Roy Keane scored 5 less than Ryan Giggs.
2. Paul Scholes scored 2 more than David Beckham.
3. Teddy Sheringham scored 4 less than David Beckham.
4. Ole Gunnar Solskjaer scored 6 less than Andy Cole.
5. Dwight Yorke scored 5 more than Andy Cole.

6. Which player scored as many goals as both Teddy Sheringham and Roy Keane altogether? _____

7. How many more goals did Andy Cole score than Paul Scholes? _____

Write the goal totals scored by these players.

8. Ole Gunnar Solskjaer and David Beckham _____

9. Dwight Yorke and Ryan Giggs _____

10. The two highest scores _____

Colour in your score on the winning players!

Answers

Adding to 10 4–5
Practise your skills
Check the jumps have been drawn correctly.
1 8 **2** 8 **3** 5 **4** 9 **5** 9

Big Match 1
1 5   **2** 10   **3** 7   **4** 8   **5** 9
6 8   **7** 9   **8** 7   **9** 10   **10** 6

Taking away 6–7
Practise your skills
A 1 11 – 3, 10 – 2, 9 – 1, 13 – 5
 2 11 – 2, 10 – 1, 14 – 5, 13 – 4, 12 – 3
 3 7 – 2, 8 – 3, 11 – 6, 10 – 5, 9 – 4
 and other possible answers
B 1 15 – 10   **2** 15 – 9

Big Match 2
1
| in | 13 | 18 | 14 | 20 | 19 |
| out | 6 | 11 | 7 | 13 | 12 |

2
| in | 20 | 15 | 16 | 19 | 13 |
| out | 12 | 7 | 8 | 11 | 5 |

Finding the difference 8–9
Practise
A 1 5   **2** 6   **3** 4
B Check answers

Big Match 3
1 3   **2** 4   **3** 7   **4** 3   **5** 5   **6** 7   **7** 3   **8** 7
9 6   **10** 7

Number facts 10–11
Practise your skills
A 1 3 + 5 = 8   5 + 3 = 8,
   8 – 3 = 5   8 – 5 = 3
 2 5 + 6 = 11   6 + 5 = 11,
   11 – 6 = 5   11 – 5 = 6
 3 9 + 3 = 12   3 + 9 = 12,
   12 – 3 = 9   12 – 9 = 3
B 9, 14, 17, 11, 6, 12, 3, 7

Big Match 4
1 8 + 9 = 17   **2** 6 + 7 = 13   **3** 9 + 6 = 15
4 12 + 8 = 20   **5** 8 + 6 = 14   **6** 13 – 8 = 5
7 17 – 8 = 9   **8** 17 – 5 = 12   **9** 8 – 5 = 3
10 13 – 5 = 8

Doubles 12–13
Practise your skills
A 2, 4, 6, 8, 10, 12, 14, 16, 18, 20
B 1 15   **2** 19   **3** 13   **4** 11   **5** 17   **6** 7   **7** 19
 8 9   **9** 17
D Yorke, Cole

Big Match 5
1 12   **2** 16   **3** 14   **4** 22   **5** 18   **6** 15   **7** 13
8 17   **9** 11   **10** 23

Missing numbers 14–15
Practise your skills
A 1 11, 4   **2** 8, 5   **3** 10, 4, 1   **4** 6, 7, 2
 5 7, 4, 3   **6** 9, 5, 6
B 1 7   **2** 5, 3   **3** 2, 8   **4** 9

Big Match 6
1 2   **2** 5   **3** 5   **4** 9   **5** 6   **6** 13   **7** 3   **8** 12
9 7   **10** 11

26

Answers

Totals 16–17
Practise your skills
A **1** 16   **2** 16   **3** 16   **4** 16
B **1** 5–0   **2** 2–0   **3** 4–0
   7–0   6–0   2–0
   1–0   5–0   7–0
   Other answers are possible

C
Other answers are possible

Big Match 7
1 6 + 4 + 2   **2** 6 + 1 + 5   **3** 9 + 1 + 2
4 8 + 1 + 3   **5** 3 + 4 + 5   **6** 6 + 7 + 6
7 4 + 9 + 6   **8** 4 + 7 + 8   **9** 2 + 7 + 10
10 8 + 2 + 9
Other answers are possible

Giving change 18–19
Practise your skills
Please check that circled coins make the following totals.
1 7   **2** 15   **3** 23   **4** 19

Big Match 8
1 3p   **2** 9p   **3** 5p   **4** 6p   **5** 12p   **6** 35p
7 60p   **8** 45p   **9** 52p   **10** 28p

Decade sums............................20–21
Practise your skills
A **1** 40, 50, 80, 90, 100
  2 80, 100, 110, 140, 150
B 60 + 40 = 100   60 + 60 = 120
   80 + 30 = 110   30 + 70 = 100
   20 + 70 = 90   50 + 30 = 80
   40 + 40 = 80   40 + 50 = 90
   70 + 50 = 120   60 + 50 = 110

Big Match 9
1 70   **2** 70   **3** 90   **4** 80   **5** 90   **6** 110   **7** 160
8 120   **9** 110   **10** 160

Money 22–23
Practise your skills
A **1** 92p   **2** 82p   **3** 53p   **4** 76p
B **1** Check answers   **2** Check answers

Big Match 10
1 50p, 20p, 1p   **2** 20p, 5p, 1p
3 20p, 20p, 5p, 2p   **4** 50p, 10p, 5p, 2p, 1p
5 20p, 10p, 1p, Other answers are possible
6 32p   **7** 74p   **8** 69p   **9** 29p   **10** 53p

Solving problems 24–25
Practise your skills
A **1** 18   **2** 14
B Check answers
C Check answers
D Check answers
E Check answers

Big Match 11
1 5   **2** 11   **3** 5   **4** 18   **5** 29   **6** Ryan Giggs
7 13   **8** 27   **9** 39   **10** 53

27

Collect the set

Collect all 6 books and be an English and Maths champion.

Manchester United English

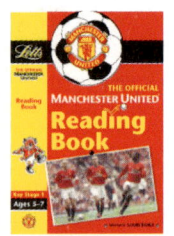

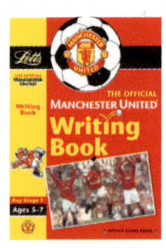

Louis Fidge

Manchester United Maths

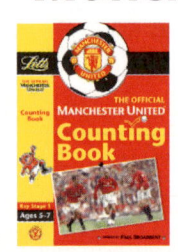

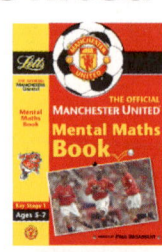

Paul Broadbent

For all the latest news, views and information on

MANCHESTER UNITED®

visit the official Manchester United website:

www.ManUtd.com

Manchester United Plc, Sir Matt Busby Way, Old Trafford, Manchester M16 0RA

Letts Educational, The Chiswick Centre, 414 Chiswick High Road, London W4 5TF
Tel: 020 8996 3333 Fax: 020 8742 8390 E-mail: mail@lettsed.co.uk
Website: www.letts-education.com

Every effort has been made to trace copyright holders and obtain their permission for the use of copyright material. The authors and publishers will gladly receive information enabling them to rectify any error or omission in subsequent editions.

All facts are correct at time of going to press.

Published 2001

Text © Letts Educational Ltd. Published under license from Manchester United Football Club, Video Collection International Limited and Carlton Books Limited. All Trade Marks related to Manchester United Football Club are used with the permission of Manchester United Football Club, Video Collection International Limited and Carlton Books Limited.
Author: Paul Broadbent
Editorial and Design: Moondisks Ltd, Cambridge
Illustrations: Joel Morris
Our thanks to Mark Wylie (MUFC museum curator) and John Peters (MUFC official photographer) for supplying material and their cooperation in the production of these books.

All rights reserved. No part of this publication may be reproduced, stored in a retrieval system, or transmitted, in any form or by any means, electronic, mechanical, photocopying, recording or otherwise, without the prior permission of Letts Educational.

British Library Cataloguing in Publication Data
A CIP record for this book is available from the British Library.

ISBN 1-85805-974-7

Printed in Italy.

Letts Educational Limited is a member of Granada Learning Limited, part of the Granada Media Group.